Raleigh

Shakespeare

Byron

Chaucer

A Ladybird Book
Series 633

This clearly written and beautifully illustrated book tells about the fascinating subject of heraldry, which is concerned not only with the romantic chivalry of the past but is also a very colourful part of our life today.

You will learn how to read a coat-of-arms, which can be a heraldic pictorial record of a family, city or school etc., and to appreciate that with its attractive and varied decorations, emblems and mythical creatures, heraldry provides interest and enjoyment in many spheres of our daily life.

The publishers wish to acknowledge the assistance of The Heraldry Society, 28 Museum Street, London, W.C.1, when preparing this book.

Learning about
heraldry

by A. E. PRIESTLEY
with illustrations by B. H. ROBINSON

Publishers: Ladybird Books Ltd . Loughborough
Printed in England

Preventing confusion

Have you ever thought how much life has been simplified by the use of different colours, numbers and other distinguishing methods? For example, it would be very difficult to organise public transport without different bus numbers. And imagine a football match with all the players of both teams dressed exactly alike! They would often be playing against the members of their own team and mistakenly helping the opposing side. So every team has its own colours—Aston Villa claret and blue, Arsenal red and white, Wolverhampton Wanderers old gold and black, and so on. On each player's back there is also a number.

Similarly, in international motor-racing, a colour is painted on the cars of each competing country—Great Britain green, France blue, Italy red, etc.—to avoid confusion.

Badges or emblems too are used to ensure easy recognition. Emblems were used for this purpose by Ancient Egyptians, Chinese and Japanese. *Totems* were carved in gay colours on totem poles by the Red Indian tribes of North America.

Today some county cricket clubs have interesting badges. The White Rose of Yorkshire and the Red Rose of Lancashire remind us of the Wars of the Roses 500 years ago, and the match between them is still called the Battle of the Roses.

0 7214 0369 7

More about emblems

The cricket badge of Kent County is the White Horse of the Saxons; that of Somerset is the Dragon of Wessex, which was the emblem on Harold's standard at the Battle of Hastings in 1066. Essex is represented by three swords (*seaxes*), and Glamorgan by the Welsh daffodil. England cricketers wear a cap and blazer of navy blue, with a badge showing the three lions of England surmounted by a crown. The Australian players wear green caps and blazers with the arms of their country shown between a kangaroo and an emu.

Distinctive devices are employed in many other ways. Inn signs are an example. The White Hart represents Richard II, The Feathers represents the Black Prince, The Red Lion was the emblem of John of Gaunt, and The Bear and Ragged Staff represents the Earl of Warwick. Some inn signs, like The George and Dragon and Robin Hood, refer to mythology and folk-lore, while others concern trades—The Wheatsheaf for bakers, The Three Horseshoes for blacksmiths, and The Green Man possibly for gamekeepers.

The Scottish clans have their own tartans of interwoven colours and often a plant emblem as well; e.g. juniper for Murray, whortleberry for Macleod of Lewis, gorse for Sinclair and periwinkle for Brodie.

Glamorgan Cricket Badge

Middlesex Cricket Badge

RED LION

WHITE HART

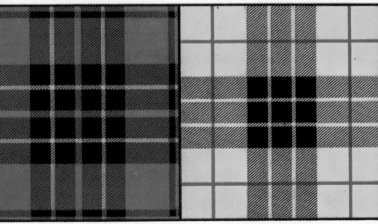

Clan Brodie of Brodie

Clan Macleod of Lewis

Symbols and badges for all

Flags have been in use from the earliest times, in battles or on ceremonial occasions, as the symbols of nations and rulers.

The United States flag has 13 red and white stripes and 50 stars on a blue ground, representing the 13 original states and the 50 states of today. The blue ensign of Australia has the white Commonwealth Star beneath the British Union flag; the five smaller stars represent the Southern Cross constellation.

Many organisations adopt a badge for identification. They include the various branches of H.M. Forces, Police, Nurses, Women's Royal Voluntary Services, the Rotary Club, Boy Scouts, The Automobile Association, societies and clubs connected with all kinds of cultural activities, such as art, music, youth-hostelling, bird-watching, cycling, sailing, angling and athletics. Most schools have a badge.

All such world-wide methods of distinguishing are really associated with a fascinating subject called heraldry. This is not only a science and an art, but a living and interesting part of history, and is governed by very definite and strict rules.

Canada

Australia

Ireland

The Netherlands

Scouts

Guides

R.N. Vice-Admiral

Army Sergeant

R.A.F. Squadron Leader

Early warfare and the Wars of the Cross

In very early warfare, before the use of distinctive colours and badges, it was extremely difficult to tell friend from foe. This must have led to great confusion and many disasters. As you can see from the famous Bayeux Tapestry depicting the Battle of Hastings, the Norman knights wore a type of armour similar to that of the Saxons, had nose-pieces on their helmets and carried long, oval-shaped shields as did their Saxon enemies. The Normans used cavalry, but when the soldiers were on foot it was not easy to tell the Normans from the Saxons.

Later on, in the Crusades, or Wars of the Cross, during the time of Richard I, the Christians fought the Mohammedans in the Holy Land to free Jerusalem. The various crusading armies came from England, France, Germany, Italy and Austria, and all needed a particular sign to show that they were fighting for the same cause. To the Christian knights, the Cross in different forms was the obvious choice. On page 13 two kinds are illustrated.

The 8-pointed Maltese Cross was the badge of the Knights Templars, who protected pilgrims travelling to Jerusalem. They used the Cross red on white. The same Cross was used silver on black by the Knights Hospitallers of St. John of Jerusalem, or Knights of Malta.

A section of the Bayeaux tapestry

The Crusades and the beginning of coats-of-arms

The silver on black Maltese Cross, shown opposite, is still the badge of the St. John Ambulance Association today. The arms of the Crusader Kings of Jerusalem consisted of one large and four small crosses of gold on a silver shield, which probably represent Christ and the four evangelists.

Eventually all the various bodies of Christian crusading knights, British and foreign, wore crosses of different shapes and patterns. You may like to find out about these from other books. You will also find many variations of the Cross used as emblems throughout heraldry (see back endpaper).

As a knight in full armour was completely hidden even to his face, which was covered by a *vizor* (the movable mask portion of his helmet), he wore over his armour a long, flowing coat or *surcoat* decorated with his armorial bearings, so that he might be recognised easily. This was known as his coat-of-arms, and is the origin of the term. The same bearings were displayed on his shield and horsecloth.

Besides ensuring that the knight would be clearly recognisable, the coat-of-arms also served another useful purpose in protecting him from the full force of the heat of the sun of the Holy Land, which would otherwise have made his armour even more uncomfortable and exhausting.

Knights Templars

Knights Hospitallers

Crusader Kings
of Jerusalem

The heralds

Heralds have been employed from very early times. In Ancient Greece they were used to proclaim the victors at the Olympic Games, and in Ancient Rome they made declarations of war. In the early Middle Ages the Chief Herald was called the Marshal. In those days, when it was the custom for the King himself to go to war, it was the Marshal's duty to *marshal* the army in groups with their banners and coats-of-arms.

In the Age of Chivalry of the Middle Ages in England, the heralds were in charge of the tournaments, or jousts, between knights. It was the heralds' duty to *blazon* (describe) the device of each knight taking part.

As time went on, it was found necessary to keep written records of the different coats-of-arms to avoid confusion—and so that they might be handed down from generation to generation. Because the heralds had to deal with this matter, it became known as *heraldry*. Later, a College of Heralds, or College of Arms, was established in London in the reign of Richard III, with the Earl Marshal as its Head. The office of Earl Marshal has remained in the family of the Duke of Norfolk to the present day.

Grades of Heraldic Officers

The Heraldic Officers include:

(a) **Kings-of-Arms:** Garter (Principal King-of-Arms and of the Order of the Garter), Clarenceux (having jurisdiction over lands below the River Trent), Norroy and Ulster (having jurisdiction over lands above the River Trent and over Northern Ireland). Scotland has its own independent authority in the person of Lord Lyon, King-of-Arms.

(b) **Heralds:** Windsor, Richmond, York, Chester, Somerset, Lancaster. Scotland — Albany, Marchmont and Rothesay. There is also a Wales Herald Extraordinary and an independent Chief Herald of Ireland (Eire).

(c) **Pursuivants:** Rouge-Croix (from the Red Cross of St. George), Blue-Mantle (from the blue coat of Edward III), Rouge-Dragon (from the Red Dragon of Wales), and Portcullis (from a badge of Henry VII, which bore a portcullis). Scotland—Carrick, Unicorn and Kintyre.

Each of these officers wears a *tabard* or short surcoat, with the Royal Arms embroidered on the back, front and sleeves. The tabard of a King-of-Arms is of velvet, that of a Herald is of satin, and that of a Pursuivant is of silk damask. The Heraldic Officers are always present at royal or state ceremonies. The Heralds' announcements are preceded by a fanfare from the trumpeters who accompany them.

Norroy King-of-Arms making an announcement

State Trumpeter, Household Cavalry

A tournament

Try to picture the thrilling pageantry of this popular medieval outdoor entertainment.

A green meadow sloped down to the fighting space called the *lists*, and at the meadow gates the scene was gay with heralds and trumpeters. Galleries alongside accommodated important spectators, including the enthroned Sovereign, with the Tournament Queen opposite. Others watched from the banks.

At one end of the lists were the splendid pavilions of the Knights Challengers; the opposing knights occupied an enclosure at the other end. Refreshment tents were behind.

Combats called *jousts*, began the day. The trumpets sounded, the heralds proclaimed the rules and announced the arms of the contestants. Amid cheers, the first six knights, lances raised, rode up to the Challengers' pavilions. Each chose his opponent by touching a Challenger's shield with his lance tip, and the combatants then took up their positions at each end (and on opposite sides) of a wooden barrier running down the centre of the lists. After another fanfare, a Challenger furiously charged his opponent. To win, a knight had to break his lance against his adversary's shield or crest, or unhorse him. The lances used were, of course, blunt—not pointed.

If all the opposing knights were defeated, others rode to meet the Challengers, until only one knight remained mounted, to be proclaimed Champion. He was crowned with flowers by the Tournament Queen and presented with his prize — a jewelled-sheathed sword and a noble steed. The day then ended with revelry.

On the second day, the real *tourney* took place. This was a general battle or 'mêlée', in which the weapons were swords with blunted edges, and there were no barriers between the contestants.

At one time sharp swords, clubs called *maces*, and battle-axes were used in tournaments. Later, they were replaced by safer weapons.

On this second day there were two larger parties of knights opposing each other, one led by the victor of the previous day, the other by the runner-up.

The trumpets sounded and the tourney began with the two parties of knights charging each other at full speed. Amid clashing of swords, the knights manoeuvred and turned their horses to avoid their adversaries' blows. This was the origin of the word *tournament*, which means a *turning about*. No doubt knights rolled to the ground, but others returned again and again to the attack, until the Sovereign gave the signal to cease and, with a final fanfare, the tourney ended.

The Champion was then crowned, by the Tournament Queen, with the laurel chaplet of honour, and he received a gleaming suit of armour as his reward.

Later the same day, or perhaps on a third day, popular amusements—archery, wrestling and bull-baiting were arranged, and the whole tournament concluded with general feasting and merrymaking.

A coat-of-arms

From the illustration opposite, it is easy to imagine how a coat-of-arms may have originated.

Today, coats-of-arms are found in all sorts of places —castles, churches, town halls, on public transport, in building societies, banks, offices and schools. Some of these are not true heraldic coats-of-arms, but merely elaborate badges. Genuine lawful arms are granted by the authority of the officers of the College of Arms and are generally designed by them.

The building-up of a coat-of-arms is quite difficult, as it must be an accurate pictorial record of what is represented. Sometimes details may have to be traced back for hundreds of years.

Special technical terms are used to describe the different features. Heraldry has its own language, built up mainly from Norman-French, Latin and early English. Because heraldry first came to us from France through Germany, some of its terms are also ancient German, so it is truly a mixture of languages.

The background of a coat-of-arms is a shield (*escutcheon*), which may be one of various shapes. If the owner is an unmarried lady or a widow, it is diamond-shaped and called a *lozenge*.

The surface of this shield or lozenge is termed the *field*.

Crest

Helmet

Wreath

Mantling

Shield

Mantling

★ VICTORY ★

Motto or
War-cry

Tinctures

When designing arms, certain so-called *colours*, *metals* and *furs* are used. There are five principal colours *(tinctures)*—*gules* (red), *azure* (blue), *sable* (black), *vert* (green) and *purpure* (purple). The metals are—*or* (gold or yellow) and *argent* (silver or white). The two most common furs are *ermine* (black on white), and *vair* (silver or white, and blue to represent grey squirrel). There are several other varieties of these two furs.

A method has been devised of indicating all these tinctures by patterns of dots and lines *(hatching, as illustrated)*, instead of colours, if the coat-of-arms is shown in black and white.

One of the rules of heraldry is that a metal shall not be placed on a metal, nor a colour on a colour, nor a fur on a fur. The reason for this is that a colour resting on a metal stands out more clearly than a colour on a colour or a metal on a metal. One of the few exceptions to this rule is found in the shield of the Crusader Kings of Jerusalem (gold crosses on a silver background), which you have already seen. The reason for its exception is that this shield, because of its particularly sacred nature, should be distinctive in some way from any other.

METALS	Or—gold or yellow	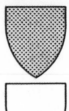
	Argent—silver or white	
COLOURS	Gules—red 	
	Azure—blue	
	Sable—black	
	Vert—green	
	Purpure—purple	
FURS	Vair	Ermine 

Divisions and decorations of shields

Terms and rules

The top part of a shield is called the *chief*, the bottom is the *base*, the centre is the *fesse* and the upper centre is the *honour point*.

The part of the shield which protects the right of the wearer is known as the dexter side, from the Latin word *dexter* meaning right. The part which covers his left is called the sinister side, from the Latin *sinister* meaning left.

The surface or field of the shield may be *charged* in different ways by bands or stripes known as *ordinaries*. Examples such as the chief, the pale, the bend, the bend sinister, the fesse, the chevron, the cross and the saltire are illustrated opposite. The field may be divided in a similar way with regular and irregular lines (see page 36).

Any decoration on a shield, such as the ordinaries already mentioned, is called a charge. All kinds of attractive and interesting charges may be used to decorate a shield—flowers, leaves, shells, birds, animals, etc.

Strange mythical creatures are used in heraldry—the dragon, the unicorn, the griffin, which is half lion and half eagle, that immortal bird the phoenix and the royal inherited beasts described on page 32.

Chief

Honour Point

Fesse Point

Base

DEXTER SINISTER

Chief Pale Bend Bend Sinister

Fesse Chevron Cross Saltire

ORDINARIES

Tudor rose

Trefoil

Mullet

Escallop

fleur-de-lis

Boar's Head proper

Eagle displayed

Dragon rampant

CHARGES

Marshalling, quartering, cadency and history in shields

The arrangement of more than one coat-of-arms on a shield is known as *marshalling*. An example is seen in the arms of England and France on the shield of Margaret of France, second queen of the English Edward I. When the shield is divided into four parts, this is called *quartering*. If two sets of arms are to be shown, e.g. the arms of a man's family and those of his mother's family, the more important one is shown in the first and fourth quarters, the other in the second and third quarters. It is a rule that no quarter must be left blank.

Additional devices introduced into arms, to distinguish different members of the same family, are called *marks of cadency*. For instance, a crescent denotes the second son and a mullet the third.

A shield may often illustrate an interesting event in history, as in the two shields of the Howards, the family of the Duke of Norfolk. The first shows the family device before the Battle of Flodden in 1513; the second, the family arms after 1513, has an added shield bearing a demi-lion pierced through the mouth by an arrow. This addition is called an *augmentation*. It refers to the defeat and slaying of James IV of Scotland by Thomas Howard, Duke of Norfolk, at Flodden.

Margaret of France

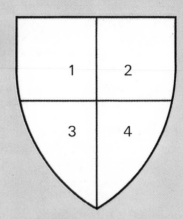

Quartering

Eldest son

label

Second son

crescent

Third son

mullet

Fourth son

martlet

Fifth son

annulet

MARKS OF CADENCY

Before 1513

Arms of Howard

After 1513

Blazoning

When we describe a shield in heraldic terms we *blazon* it. Here are the simple rules of blazon:

1. Describe the background (field) of the shield.
2. Describe the principal charge placed directly on to the field.
3. Describe the lesser charges on the field.
4. Describe any lesser charges placed on the principal charge.

The small shields illustrated opposite are blazoned as follows:

(a) Sable, a bend or
(b) Or, a bend sinister gules
(c) Argent, a chevron azure
(d) Gules, a fesse argent
(e) Vert, a saltire or
(f) Or, on a chevron sable between three leopards' faces gules, three castles argent.

The shield bearing the Royal Arms is quartered, with the three lions of England in the *first* and *fourth* quarters, the lion of Scotland in the *second*, and the Irish harp in the *third*. The blazon of this shield would be:

Quarterly, 1 and 4, gules, three lions passant guardant in pale or; 2, or a lion rampant gules within a double tressure flory-counter-flory gules; 3, azure, a harp or, stringed argent.

The above in ordinary language:

Quartered: in the first and fourth quarters, on a red ground, three gold lions walking and looking out arranged vertically; in the second quarter, on a gold ground, a red lion erect and looking forward in a frame decorated with fleur-de-lis; in the third quarter on a blue ground a gold harp with silver strings.

a.

b.

c.

d.

e.

f.

The Royal Arms

The Royal Beasts

The ten Royal Beasts are taken from heraldic devices of the Queen's ancestors. The models made for her coronation were later removed from Westminster Abbey to Kew Gardens. They are:

1. THE LION OF ENGLAND, from the earliest known coat-of-arms dating from Henry I.

2. THE UNICORN OF SCOTLAND, which had become the Scottish Royal Beast by 1426. When James VI of Scotland became James I of England, the Unicorn joined the Lion as a supporter in the Royal Arms.

3. THE RED DRAGON OF WALES, which Henry VII added to his standard and bore on Bosworth Field.

4. THE GRIFFIN OF EDWARD III, who adopted it for his private seal.

5. THE WHITE LION OF MORTIMER, dating from Edward IV, who inherited it through the powerful nobles, the Mortimers.

6. THE YALE OF BEAUFORT, a mythical animal with the appearance of a goat and the grace of a deer. Henry VII inherited it from his mother, heiress of John Beaufort, Earl of Somerset.

7. THE WHITE GREYHOUND OF RICHMOND, inherited by Henry VII from his father, Edmund Tudor, Earl of Richmond.

8. THE FALCON OF THE PLANTAGENETS, chosen by Edward III, because of his love of hawking.

9. THE BLACK BULL OF CLARENCE, which derived from Anne of Clarence, grandmother of Edward IV.

10. THE WHITE HORSE OF HANOVER, introduced into the Royal Arms when the Elector of Hanover became George I of England.

1.

2.

3.

4.

5.

6.

7.

8.

9.

10.

Outer decorations of a coat-of-arms

THE CREST is an object at the top of a coat-of-arms, originally worn on the knight's helmet, perhaps as a token given him by his lady. It rests upon a wreath, cap, or coronet. The wreath represents the twisted scarf binding the crest to the helmet.

THE HELMET shows the rank of the owner of the arms. A Sovereign's helmet is gold and faces to the front; that of a peer is silver with gold bars facing sideways; a baronet's or knight's helmet is steel without bars, the vizor raised and facing to the front; that of an untitled person is also steel, the vizor closed and facing sideways.

THE MANTLING hanging from the helmet represents the cloth originally protecting the crusading knight from the sun. The raggedness of its appearance probably indicates the sword cuts in it, received in battle.

THE SUPPORTERS are figures of animals or persons placed on either side of the shields of important personages or towns. They may originally have represented the knight's pages who guarded his shield before the fray.

THE MOTTO is usually a short sentence or phrase to serve as a rule and encouragement, such as *Stand fast*, *Victory or Death*. It probably originates from the medieval knight's war-cry.

A complete coat-of-arms including the shield and all these features is called an *achievement*.

HELMETS

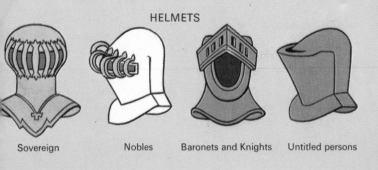

Sovereign   Nobles   Baronets and Knights   Untitled persons

FULL ACHIEVEMENT OF ROYAL COAT-OF-ARMS

Crest

Crown

Helmet

Mantling

Supporter

Supporter

Garter

Blazoned Shield

Motto ("God and my right")

Civic heraldry

This is heraldry which is connected with towns and cities. The arms of many of them tell something of their history or activities. The goat and ram as supporters in Bradford's arms refer to its woollen industry. In the arms of Birmingham, two of its most prominent families are represented—the de Bermingham family by the gold lozenges on blue and the divided quarter of gold and red. The ermine fesse is taken from the arms of the Calthorpe family. The crest and supporters indicate the city's activities in industry and art. The arms are blazoned as follows:

Quarterly first and fourth azure a bend of five lozenges or, second and third per pale indented or and gules, over all a fesse ermine thereon a Mural* Crown or. For the Crest, on a Wreath or and azure, a Mural* Crown, issuant therefrom a dexter Arm embowed the hand holding a hammer all proper†, the Motto *Forward*.

The Supporters are blazoned as follows:

On the dexter side a Man habited as a Smith (representing Industry) holding in the dexter hand a Hammer resting on an Anvil all proper and on the sinister side a Female Figure (representing Art) proper vested Argent wreathed round the temples with Laurel Vert tied by a Ribband Gules holding in the dexter hand, resting on the Shield, a Book bound also Gules and in the sinister a Painter's Palette Or with two Brushes proper.

---

* *A Mural (brickwork) Crown denotes Civic Arms.*
† *In natural (not heraldic) colours.*

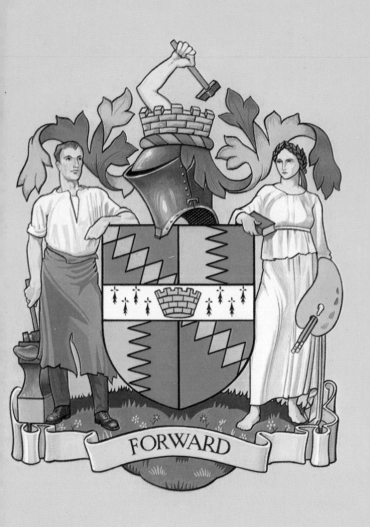

FORWARD

Scholastic heraldry

The coats-of-arms of schools and colleges often give a clue to their founders. The branch of dates in the crest of Rugby School refers to its founder, Lawrence Sheriff, a warden of the Grocers' Company. The silver lion in the arms of Harrow School is a pun on the name of its founder, John Lyon. In Eton College's coat-of-arms, the three white lilies, emblems of purity, symbolise the school's dedication to the Virgin Mary. The lion of England and fleur-de-lis of France indicate its royal foundation by Henry VI.

Certain features in the arms of a school may also indicate the type of school. George Heriot's School in Edinburgh has, as its crest, a cornucopia, or horn of plenty, showing its origin as a charity school for the maintenance of destitute orphans.

Other devices in school arms refer to some feature in the locality of the school, e.g. the crest of silver-birch leaves in the arms of Birkenhead School is said to be derived from the local birch-clad headland.

The pigeons in the arms of Dean Close School, Cheltenham, which are also in that borough's coat-of-arms, refer to the legend of the discovery of Cheltenham's mineral waters as a result of pigeons flocking round a spring.

George Heriot's School crest

Rugby School crest

Eton College

Birkenhead School crest

Harrow School

Dean Close School

The Knightly Orders

At important royal and state ceremonies, not only the heraldic officers are present, but also the chief officers of the various Orders of Chivalry or Knighthood in full dress.

In the early Middle Ages, before a young man could become a knight, he had to *win his spurs* and was then knighted as a reward. The Sovereign touching him on the shoulder with a drawn sword and bidding him 'Rise Sir Knight', was termed the *accolade*. Later, knighthood was attended by solemn religious ceremonies. Certain knights joined together in companies, or Orders, and many new Orders of Knighthood were established as time went on, each with its own rules and emblems.

The most famous of our Knightly Orders is The Most Noble Order of the Garter, founded by Edward III at about 1350. There is a story that at a banquet given by the King at Windsor Castle, the blue silk garter of one of the noble ladies fell off. To spare her embarrassment, the King himself gallantly picked up the garter and fastened it round his own leg, with the words 'Honi soit qui mal y pense' (Shame be to him who thinks evil of it). So, it is said, originated the emblem and motto of this famous Order, which has the Sovereign as its Head.

Another Order of great distinction is The Most Honourable Order of the Bath, named from the cleansing ceremony which the medieval knight underwent to signify the pure life he vowed to lead.

The GARTER is fastened like this and worn below the left knee.

The Order of the Garter

The Order of the Bath

CEREMONIAL DRESS

Other Noble Orders

The Most Ancient and Noble Order of the Thistle is a Scottish Order, and Lord Lyon, King-of-Arms, is one of its officers.

The Most Distinguished Order of St. Michael and St. George honours persons for service overseas and in foreign affairs.

The Most Excellent Order of the British Empire, established by George V, is conferred on persons who have served the country or Empire in some special way.

These are but a few of the many British Knightly Orders which exist today. Each individual honour ceases on the death of the holder.

Peers are also members of an Order in the realm, ranking as follows: duke, marquess, earl, viscount and baron. Most of these titles are hereditary, that is, handed down from father to son. Some life peers are now created for special services to the State, but their titles are not hereditary. All peers may sit in the House of Lords.

Archbishops and bishops are also peers and sit in the House of Lords. They are called the Lords Spiritual, while the other peers are the Lords Temporal. The titles of officers of the Church are not hereditary.

The Order of the Thistle

The Order of St. Patrick

CEREMONIAL DRESS

Sovereign's children, brothers and sisters (except Heir Apparent)

Duke

Marquess

Earl

Viscount

Baron

CORONETS

Other Noble Orders *(continued)*

All members of knightly orders and the peerage wear their own particular *insignia*—badges and emblems—at a Royal ceremony such as a coronation, but the insignia of royalty—the Crown Jewels or *Regalia*—are the most magnificent of all. Most of the originals were unfortunately broken up during Cromwell's Commonwealth, but new insignia were produced at the restoration of Charles II. They are stored in the Jewel House of the Tower of London and include:

THE CROWNS—the most sacred is St. Edward's Crown, named after Edward the Confessor and used for the actual crowning of the monarch; the Imperial State Crown, used on other State occasions, is the most valuable.

THE ORB—with its surmounting cross, the symbol of Christianity ruling the world.

THE SCEPTRES—emblems of royal dignity.

THE SWORDS of State—emblems of spiritual and temporal justice and mercy. The sword of mercy is called *Curtana*, meaning *shortened*, because it is unpointed.

THE SPURS of St. George, emblem of knightly chivalry.

THE RING, with five rubies on a large sapphire, representing the Cross of St. George upon that of St. Andrew.

THE BRACELETS, of solid gold, richly enamelled with emblems.

THE AMPULLA, an eagle-shaped, gold flask for containing the anointing oil.

THE ANOINTING SPOON, of silver gilt.

St. Edward´s Crown

Imperial State Crown

Sceptre

Orb

Ampulla

Anointing Spoon

Flags and banners

No royal or state pageant is complete without its setting of flags and banners. They are used as special symbols of nations, services or persons and are most effective for heraldic display, their brilliant colours fluttering gracefully in the breeze.

Three kinds of flags date from the Middle Ages: the pennon, the banner, and the standard.

The pennon, triangular in shape, pointed or swallow-tailed, was the symbol of the ordinary knight, bearing his device and displayed upon his lance. The banner and the standard were the flags of kings, princes, great nobles and anyone having a coat-of-arms. The banner was square or oblong, with the owner's coat-of-arms displayed over the whole surface. In olden times, if a knight had shown exceptional bravery, he was promoted on the battlefield. His pennon, with the point cut off, formed the higher emblem of the banner. The standard was long and tapering, with badges and mottoes spread across its surface. The Royal Standard, as it is called, is not really a standard, but a banner, as you will see from the illustration. It bears the Royal Arms, and certain differences appear in the personal banners of different members of the Royal Family.

Today, the national flags of Great Britain are the Union Jack (more correctly called the *Union flag*) and the various Ensigns, which are described and explained in detail on page 48.

Pennon

Modern pennant of a
Royal Navy Commodore

Standard of Henry Bolingbroke

The Royal Banner

The Union Jack and the Ensigns

Here is one of the possible explanations of the term *Union Jack*. *Jack* comes from the French, *Jacques* (James). It was King James I who ordered the production of the first Union Jack. The term *Union* was used because England and Scotland were united in his reign.

The English flag showed the Cross of St. George in red on a white background. The Scottish flag bore the white saltire, or diagonal Cross of St. Andrew on a field of blue. The first combined flag was formed by laying the red Cross of St. George, with a narrow white border, over the white Cross of St. Andrew with its background of blue. Later, when Ireland also was united to England, the red saltire Cross of St. Patrick was introduced into the flag in 1801.

The Union Jack appears in the top left-hand (hoist) corner of each of the three Ensigns. The White Ensign has a field of white. This is the flag of the British Royal Navy, the Dominions' Navies and the Royal Yacht Squadron. The Blue Ensign has a blue background. It is flown by the Royal Naval Reserve and certain merchant vessels with naval reservists in their crews. The Red Ensign (nicknamed the *Red Duster*) has a plain red ground, and is carried by all ships which do not fly the White or Blue Ensign.

St. George

St. Andrew

St. Patrick

The first Union Flag 1606

The Union Flag since 1801

White Ensign

Blue Ensign

Red Ensign

Tracing ancestors

Tracing a person's descent from ancestors is called *genealogy*. The science of genealogy is an important part of heraldry.

When building up a family tree, all family papers are searched for any old birth, baptism, marriage and death certificates and wills. The General Register at Somerset House in London is consulted for records as far back as July 1837.

Helpful information can be obtained from the census returns of 1841, 1851 and 1861. These are kept at the Public Record Office in London. Some public libraries now contain genealogical records and census returns which may be studied free of charge.

Finally, it may be necessary to study the parish registers of baptisms, marriages and burials in churches in the districts in which ancestors lived.

It is possible to have a pedigree traced by a qualified member of the Society of Genealogists but this may prove rather expensive. If a family has an armorial bearing, the College of Arms will trace its ancestry for a fee.

Apart from the genealogical interest of their parish registers, our churches have much of heraldic interest to offer in the stained glass windows, banners, and brass and stone effigies of the early knights to be found there.

Heraldic banners in Westminster Abbey

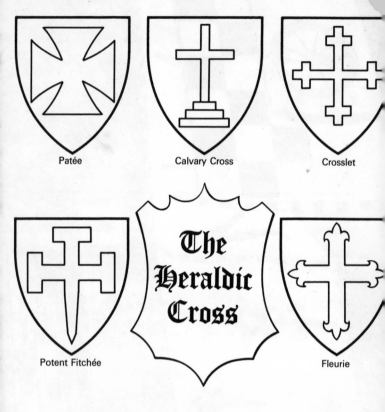

Patée

Calvary Cross

Crosslet

The Heraldic Cross

Potent Fitchée

Fleurie

Moline

Couped

Botonée